Overcoming
Guilt, Grief
& Regret

A Caregiver's Guide

Dedication

To all the caregivers and their families
who are experiencing guilt, grief and regret
as a result of caring for those you love.

You give care because you love the people
you care for, even when they don't recognize it.
Rest assured you are doing the best you can.

Your sacrifice is more precious than you know.
Caregivers DO Matter.

Contents

"There are only four kinds of people in the world,

Those who have been *caregivers*.

Those who are currently *caregivers*.

Those who will be *caregivers*,

and those who will need a *caregiver*.

— *Rosalynn Carter*

INTRODUCTION

As a full-time caregiver, I never thought how enormous the task would be. I believed I could handle whatever came my way. After all, caregiving is merely watching over someone you know and love; making sure they are safe and comfortable. Boy was I wrong! The truth is the invisible emotional toll it takes becomes very visible in time. It is often too much to bear.

Caregivers are ordinary people who take on an extraordinary responsibility. They provide care and support to family members who are aging, ill, or disabled. Caregiving is a very demanding job, and caregivers may experience physical and emotional stress, financial struggles, and other difficult situations. Misconceptions about the role of caregiving make it difficult for those who provide care, as well as for the recipient.

The good news, however, is that we don't have to go through this dark tunnel alone. In this guide, I share stories of encouragement and instruction of how to recognize and manage these emotions.

I offer solutions to help caregivers find the support they need and how to take care of themselves, too. Simply put, we can't take care of others if we're not taking care of ourselves first.

Some of the most beneficial and intriguing features are the stories depicting caregivers' experiences. I can relate to many of them that lets me know I am not alone. We need support to recognize the bright light at the end of the tunnel—the moments of joy and love that make it all worthwhile. I urge you to acknowledge feelings of guilt, grief, and regret, especially during times when you want to give up, so you can discover ways to move beyond them.

CHAPTER 1 — WHAT IS A CAREGIVER

A caregiver or carer is a paid or unpaid member of a person's social network who helps them with activities of daily living. Since they have no specific professional training, they are often described as informal caregivers. Caregivers most commonly assist with impairments related to old age, disability, a disease, or a mental disorder.

Typical duties of a caregiver might include taking care of someone who has a chronic illness or disease; managing medications or talking to doctors and nurses on someone's behalf; helping to bathe or dress someone who is frail or disabled; or taking care of household chores, meals, or processes both formal and informal documentation related to health for someone who cannot do these things alone.

1

With an aging population in all developed societies, the role of caregiver has been increasingly recognized as an important one, both functionally and economically. Many organizations that provide support for persons with disabilities have developed various forms of support for carers as well.

One must recognize that it is a calling with a higher purpose. It requires tremendous strength, empathy, compassion, and patience. It's not an easy task, but it's a gift that can bring joy and fulfillment to you and the person you care for.

Caregiving is not just a job, but a calling. Caregiving may not be the most glamorous job, but it is undoubtedly one of the most purposeful. The act of providing care can give you a sense of meaning and purpose that few other jobs can offer. Every task, no matter how small, has the potential to create a positive impact in the life of the person you care for.

A Passionate Caregiver

"What I love about being a caregiver is the ability to make a positive impact on people's lives," said Victoria.

Victoria always knew that caregiving was her calling. As a little girl, she was known for her nurturing and caring personality. She used to take care of her siblings, and they always felt well taken care of by her. Victoria felt that she could use her strengths to make a positive impact on people's lives, and caregiving would allow her to do so.

Victoria's journey to becoming a caregiver began with taking classes and earning certifications. She learned the importance of empathy, communication, and patience when working with patients. She understood that caregiving required more than just professional knowledge and certification. It required a warm and compassionate nature that comes naturally to her.

Victoria added that "I have a genuine passion for caregiving, and I believe that my patients need that kind of passion from me. It's about more than just providing care - it's about making a difference and improving the quality of someone's life."

Victoria landed her dream job at a local nursing home where she worked with elderly patients who needed assistance with everyday tasks. Her colleagues and patients quickly recognized her for her kind and compassionate nature. Victoria made sure to spend enough time with each patient, listening to their stories, and sharing in their joys and sorrows. She believed in treating every patient with respect, dignity, and kindness.

In Victoria's own words, "Being a caregiver is not just about providing care but also about forming connections. I believe that every patient deserves my full attention and care."

As the years went by, Victoria formed deep connections with many of her patients. She learned about their lives and listened to their stories. Her patients shared their sorrows and joys with her, and Victoria always tried to give them a sense of comfort and support.

"If you show genuine compassion for your patients, you get to understand more about their lives and what they have gone through. You get to create a bond that makes you more like a friend than just a caregiver," added Victoria.

Victoria's reputation as a caregiver quickly spread among families who needed someone to care for their loved ones. She became recognized by her colleagues and seniors for her outstanding work.

Victoria's nursing supervisor shared, "Victoria is a great member of our team. She always goes above and beyond to make sure her patients are happy and comfortable, and we couldn't ask for more from her."

Although Victoria has retired, her legacy as a caregiver lives on. Her patients remember her kindness and compassion, and the families she served are grateful for the care she provided to their loved ones.

As Victoria said, "I am proud of my work as a caregiver. I believe that being compassionate and caring is something that can stay with someone for their entire life."

In the end, Victoria's story is a testament to the power of caregiving and the impact one person can have on the lives of many. Her passion, kindness, and compassion made her a great caregiver, and her legacy will live on in the people whose lives she touched.

Some ways people become caregivers are:

There are many ways that people become caregivers. Some become caregivers out of necessity, because a loved one becomes ill, injured, or disabled and needs their help. Others may become caregivers because they feel a sense of duty or responsibility to care for an aging or ill family member.

Family caregiving: Often, family members become caregivers for a loved one who needs assistance due to a chronic illness, disability, or aging. This can include providing physical care, emotional support, and assistance with activities of daily living.

Professional caregiving: Professional caregivers are individuals who are trained to provide care to others, often in a healthcare setting. This can include nurses, home health aides, personal care assistants, and other healthcare professionals.

Volunteer caregiving: Some people become caregivers as volunteers, helping others in their community who need help. This can include visiting elderly or disabled individuals, providing transportation, or helping with errands and household tasks.

Caregiving for children: Parents and other family members may become caregivers for children who have special needs, such as developmental disabilities, chronic illnesses, or behavioral issues.

No matter how someone becomes a caregiver, it is a role that requires patience, compassion, and dedication.

Often, a caregiver will experience being unappreciated by the one they are caring for. Although they have become the primary caregiver, fulfilling the person's every need, they can often be met with hostility and sometimes physical harm. It's easy to say it is not to be taken personally, but the truth is, it still hurts.

Being a caregiver is more than just employment or a menial task to perform. There is also the joy of making a difference. Few professions can give one the opportunity to connect with others and make a difference in their lives. When you provide exceptional care, you can create a positive change in the world. Whether you're caring for a family member, friend, or stranger, the impact of your work can be immeasurable. The feeling of satisfaction that comes from making a meaningful difference in someone's life is unparalleled.

Caregiving has its costs. Many caregivers encounter intense emotions that can be unsettling for both them and those they care for. These feelings may manifest as anger, frustration, and exhaustion, along with guilt, grief, and regret.

Let's focus on the latter—guilt, grief, and regret—and explore strategies for overcoming these emotions if they arise during your caregiving journey.

How Did I Get Here?

How did I become a caregiver? Was it something I chose, or was it simply a responsibility thrust upon me? However, it was an undiscovered area of my life. I've never been down this road before.

Growing up, my mother was always the rock of our family. She was the one who took care of me when I was sick, cooked our meals, and made sure I had everything I needed. She was the one who attended every school play, teacher's conference, and sports event that I participated in.

Dad was there, but he was always too tired from working overtime and never took time off for vacations, even when he was sick. It was his dedication to taking care of the family that sent him to an early grave at age 56.

But as mom got older, things changed. Her health began to decline, and suddenly, it was my turn to take care of her, as I was the only child.

At first, it was just routine things. I would drive her to doctor's appointments, help her with her groceries, and make sure she was taking her medication on time. But as time went on, her needs grew, and so did my responsibilities.

Life has a way of rudely disrupting our journey without apologies.

It became very hard to form serious relationships, attend social events or even have time to myself. I was hampered with making sure mom was taken care of or burdened with guilt of even thinking about enjoying myself.

Now, I'm here almost every day, making sure she eats, helping her with her hygiene, and keeping her company. It's not always easy, and there are days when I feel like I'm drowning in the weight of it all. But then I think about all the things my mother did for me when I was growing up, and I know that I can't let her down now.

Being a caregiver is a hard and often thankless job, but it's also one of the most gratifying things I've ever done. It's taught me patience, compassion, and the importance of putting others before myself. And when my mother looks up at me with those tired, grateful eyes, I know that every sacrifice I've made has been worth it.

So how did I get here? I suppose it was a combination of fate, circumstance, and love. But whatever the reason, as difficult as it is, I wouldn't trade this experience for anything in the world.

CHAPTER 2 — GUILT

Guilt in full-time caregiving is the feeling of responsibility or remorse that arises when one believes or knows that they have done something wrong or failed to do something they should have done. It is often accompanied by feelings of shame, regret, and self-reproach. Guilt can stem from a variety of sources, including violating one's own moral code or societal norms, causing harm to others, or failing to meet personal or societal expectations.

Caregivers may feel guilty for a variety of reasons, such as feeling like they are not doing enough for their loved ones, feeling like they are not doing things correctly, feeling like they are not meeting their own expectations or the expectations of others, feeling like they are neglecting their own needs, or feeling like they are not doing enough to prevent their loved ones from experiencing pain, discomfort, or suffering.

It is important for caregivers to recognize that they are doing the best they can with the resources and support available to them, and to practice self-compassion and self-care to help manage these feelings. It can also be helpful for caregivers to seek support from other caregivers or professional resources to help them cope with the challenges of caregiving.

There are steps that caregivers can take to help alleviate these feelings and feel more confident in their role:

Acknowledge and accept your feelings: It's normal to feel guilty at times as a caregiver. Acknowledge your feelings and accept that they are a natural part of the caregiving experience.

Prioritize self-care: To be an effective caregiver, make sure you prioritize self-care activities, such as exercise, relaxation, and spending time with friends and family.

Seek support: It's important to have a support system in place, whether it's through a support group, therapist, or family and friends. Talking to others who have similar experiences can help you feel less alone and more understood.

Set realistic expectations: Caregiving can be overwhelming, and it's important to set realistic expectations for yourself and your loved one. Don't be too hard on yourself if you can't do everything, and don't feel guilty for needing to ask for help.

Celebrate your successes: It's important to recognize and celebrate your successes as a caregiver, no matter how small they may seem. Focusing on the positive can help you feel more confident and less guilty.

Remember that caregiving is a challenging role, and it's important to take care of yourself to be the best caregiver you can be.

Guiltless Caregiving

Linda had always been close to her aunt, Mary, so, when Mary's husband passed away and she was left alone, Linda didn't hesitate to offer her a place to stay. Now, several years later, Linda had become Mary's full-time caregiver.

Linda's days were spent preparing meals, administering medication, and assisting Mary with everything from bathing to dressing. It was a difficult and exhausting job, but Linda never complained. She loved her aunt and wanted to provide her with the best care.

However, as time went on, Linda found herself growing increasingly frustrated with Mary. No matter what Linda did, it was never enough. Mary would always find something to complain about, whether it was the food, the temperature, or the way Linda had arranged her belongings. Linda tried her best to be patient, but sometimes it became overwhelming.

One day, after a particularly difficult morning, Linda found herself sitting on the porch, tears rolling down her cheeks. She felt guilty for feeling frustrated with Mary. After all, Mary had been there for her when she was growing up. Linda knew that Mary couldn't help being the way she was, but she couldn't help feeling overwhelmed and exhausted.

Linda's daughter came out to check on her and saw her crying. She hugged her mom and sat down next to her on the porch. Linda told her daughter how guilty she felt for being frustrated with Mary, and how she didn't know how much longer she could keep up with the demands of being a caregiver.

Her daughter listened patiently and told her that it was okay to feel frustrated. It didn't mean that Linda loved Mary any less. Caregiving was a difficult and demanding job, and it was natural to feel overwhelmed at times. She also reminded Linda that taking care of herself was just as important as taking care of Mary.

Linda realized that her daughter was right. She needed to take care of herself and find ways to cope with the stress of caregiving. She started taking breaks throughout the day to do things she enjoyed, like reading or gardening. She also started going to a support group for caregivers, where she found comfort in talking to others who were going through the same thing.

Over time, Linda learned to manage her frustration and guilt. She realized that it was possible to love someone and still feel frustrated with them. Most importantly, she learned that taking care of herself was essential to being a good caregiver.

Guilt can have a significant impact on caregivers as they often experience guilt related to their role. It can also arise from difficult decisions, such as deciding to place a loved one in a care facility or making end-of-life decisions.

The emotional toll of caregiving is substantial, and guilt can contribute to feelings of stress, anxiety, and depression. Caregivers may feel as though are failing their loved one, which can lead to feelings of helplessness and frustration.

Caregivers may also experience physical effects of guilt, such as fatigue, headaches, and other stress-related symptoms. Guilt can also impact relationships with friends and family members, as caregivers may withdraw from social activities or feel like they are burdening others with their responsibilities.

It is important for caregivers to address feelings of guilt and seek support when needed. This may include talking with a trusted friend or family member, joining a support group, or seeking professional counseling. Caregivers should also prioritize self-care and take time for themselves to prevent burnout and manage stress.

Here are some tips that may help you handle guilt associated with caregiving:

Recognize that it's normal to feel guilty: It's important to understand that feeling guilty is a normal and common experience for caregivers. You're not alone in feeling this way.

Identify the source of your guilt: Try to figure out what is causing you to feel guilty. Is it because you feel like you're not doing enough? Or because you feel like you're neglecting other responsibilities? Understanding the source of your guilt can help you address it.

Talk to someone: Sharing your feelings with a trusted friend, family member, or therapist can help you process your emotions and gain a new perspective on your situation.

Practice self-compassion: Be kind to yourself and acknowledge that you're doing the best you can in a challenging situation. Treat yourself the way you would treat a friend in need. Be kind, understanding, and patient with yourself. Remind yourself that you're doing something important and valuable by caring for your loved one.

Take care of yourself: It's important to take care of your own needs and well-being, too. Make time for yourself, engage in self-care activities, and seek support when you need it.

Consider seeking professional help: If your guilt is causing significant distress or interfering with your ability to function, it may be helpful to speak with a mental health professional who can help you work through your feelings and develop coping strategies.

Overcoming caregiver guilt is about recognizing your limitations, being kind to yourself, and breaking the cycle of self-blame. Remember that you are doing enough, and your love and care are invaluable. Prioritize self-care and seek help if you need it. By taking care of yourself and seeking support when you need it, you can better manage your feelings and provide the best possible care for your loved one. Caregiving can be challenging, but with the right mind-set and support, you can overcome any obstacle.

Siblings and Guilt

It is common for siblings who do not play an active role in caring for their ailing aging parents to experience feelings of guilt. They may feel guilty for not doing enough to help their parents or for not being there for them when they needed it.

There are several ways in which siblings who don't care for ailing aging parents may express their guilt:

Apologizing: Siblings may apologize to their parents for not being there for them as much as they should have been.

Avoidance: Some siblings may avoid spending time with their parents or discussing their care, as they feel guilty about not being more involved.

Defensive behavior: Siblings who feel guilty may become defensive when their level of involvement in their parents' care is questioned.

Overcompensation: Other siblings may overcompensate by trying to make up for their lack of involvement by doing more than their fair share of caregiving tasks.

Resentment: Some siblings may feel resentful towards their siblings who are more involved in their parents' care, as they feel guilty about not doing more themselves.

Where is Frank Jr.?

Frank Jr. had always been distant from his father, Frank Sr. He had his own life and priorities, and taking care of his aging father was not one of them. Meanwhile, Frank Sr.'s health was deteriorating with each passing day, and his daughter Frances could see it all too clearly. She had given up her own career and moved her father into her home to care for him.

As the months passed, Frank Jr. became consumed with his work and personal life, neglecting to check in on his father or assist his sister in any way. Although he was aware of his sister's situation, he remained apathetic towards it.

However, Frank Sr.'s condition deteriorated to the point where he required hospitalization. Frances faithfully stayed by his side every day, but Frank Jr. was nowhere to be found.

Frank Jr. was overwhelmed with guilt. He recognized that he should have been there for his father and sister, but now it was too late. He couldn't bring himself to visit his father in the hospital, fully aware that he had let him down. He vowed to himself that he would do better once his father was discharged.

But Frank Sr.'s condition continued to deteriorate, and he eventually passed away. Frank Jr. was consumed by guilt and regret. He had missed his chance to make things right with his father and to support his sister in her time of need. He was overwhelmed by the weight of his guilt and didn't know what to do.

He confided in a close friend, who listened patiently and offered some advice. "You can't change the past, but you can change the future," the friend said. "You can't bring your father back, but you can honor his memory by being there for your family now. Reach out to your sister and see if there's anything you can do to help her. It won't undo what's been done, but it's a start."

Frank Jr. took the advice to heart and reached out to his sister. She was still grieving but appreciated the gesture. They talked for hours, and Frank Jr. listened as she recounted her experiences caring for their father. He realized how much she had sacrificed and how little he had done to support her.

"I'm sorry," he said, tears welling up in his eyes. "I should have been there for you and Dad."

Frances took his hand and squeezed it gently. "I know," she said. "But it's okay now. We can move forward from here."

Frank Jr. knew that he had a long way to go to make up for his past mistakes, but he was determined to try.

He started visiting his sister more often, helping her with chores, and spending time with her. He even started volunteering at a local senior center, hoping to make a difference in the lives of other seniors in need.

Over time, Frank Jr.'s guilt started to fade, replaced by a sense of purpose and fulfillment. He knew that he could never change the past, but he could make a difference in the present and the future. And he was determined to do just that.

In the end, Frank Jr. realized that the best way to honor his father's memory was to be there for his family and make a positive impact in the world. His journey had been difficult, but he had learned a valuable lesson: it's never too late to do the right thing.

It is important for siblings to acknowledge and address their feelings of guilt in order to move forward and provide supportive for their aging parents. This may involve engaging in open and honest conversations with both their parents and siblings about their emotions and finding opportunities to become more involved in their parents' care if feasible. Additionally, seeking the assistance of a therapist or counselor can be advantageous in working through feelings of guilt and developing strategies to manage caregiving responsibilities.

Frequently Asked Questions: (FAQ's)

What causes guilt in full-time caregivers?

Full-time caregivers may feel guilty for a variety of reasons, including a sense of inadequacy, the desire for personal time and space, and negative emotions towards the person they are caring for.

What are the effects of guilt on full-time caregivers?

Guilt can lead to physical exhaustion, mental fatigue, and emotional distress. Caregivers may experience symptoms such as headaches, body aches, and trouble sleeping.

How can full-time caregivers overcome guilt?

Caregivers can overcome guilt by re framing their perspective, seeking support, practicing self-care, and acknowledging and accepting their feelings of guilt.

What are the results of overcoming guilt for full-time caregivers?

Overcoming guilt can lead to an increase in energy, a more positive outlook, and an improved ability to handle stress. Caregivers may also feel more motivated, experience better sleep, and reengage in activities they once enjoyed.

How can full-time caregivers handle guilt effectively?

Caregivers should prioritize self-care, seek support from family and friends, participate in support groups, or consider therapy to handle guilt effectively.

CHAPTER 3 — GRIEF

Grief in a full-time caregiver is a complex emotional response to the loss and changes that can accompany caring for a loved one who is chronically ill, disabled, or dying. Caregivers may experience grief as they witness the decline of their loved one's health, as they manage the demands of caregiving, and as they confront the uncertainties and challenges of providing care.

Grief can take many forms for full-time caregivers, including feelings of sadness, anger, guilt, fear, and frustration. Caregivers may also experience a sense of isolation or loneliness, as the demands of caregiving can make it difficult to maintain social connections or engage in activities that provide emotional support.

The Effects of Grief

Long-term grief can have a significant impact on caregivers who provide emotional and physical support to a loved one who is experiencing loss. Here are some of the effects of long-term grief on caregivers:

Emotional distress: Grief can cause intense emotional distress, including feelings of sadness, anger, guilt, and helplessness. Caregivers may experience these emotions themselves, or they may be affected by the emotions of the person they are caring for.

Physical symptoms: Grief can also cause physical symptoms such as fatigue, insomnia, loss of appetite, and headaches. Caregivers who are experiencing grief may struggle to take care of their own physical needs, which can lead to further health problems.

Social isolation: Caregivers may become socially isolated as they spend more time caring for their loved one and less time engaging in activities and relationships outside of their caregiving role.

Financial strain: Grief can also have financial consequences, particularly if the person being cared for had significant medical expenses or was the primary breadwinner in the household. Caregivers may need to take time off from work or reduce their hours to provide care, which can lead to a loss of income.

Burnout: Caregivers who are experiencing long-term grief may be at risk for burnout, which can manifest as physical and emotional exhaustion, cynicism, and a sense of detachment from the caregiving role.

It is important for caregivers to prioritize their own mental and physical health during the grieving process. This may involve seeking support from friends and family, joining a support group, or seeking professional counseling. Taking time for self-care activities such as exercise, meditation, or hobbies can also help caregivers manage the effects of long-term grief.

Overcome by Grief

Betty had always been a caring person. As a child, she would take in stray animals and nurse them back to health, and as an adult, she became a caregiver for the elderly and disabled. But nothing could have prepared her for the emotional journey she was about to embark on when her son Derrick was diagnosed with a rare genetic disease at the age of 5.

The first few years were hard, but Betty was determined to give her son the best care possible. She learned everything she could about the disease, attended support groups, and even started her own blog to share her experiences and connect with other parents in similar situations. She utilized her investments in order to quit her job to become a full-time caregiver, and her days were filled with doctor's appointments, physical therapy, and medication management.

Despite the challenges, Betty found joy in the small moments with her son. They would play board games, watch movies, and take walks together. Derrick was a bright and curious child, full of questions about the world around him. Betty did her best to answer them, even if she didn't always have the answers.

As years passed, Betty watched her son's condition deteriorate. He became wheelchair-bound and required a feeding tube. As his physical abilities declined, Derrick's spirit remained strong. He was always quick with a joke or a witty remark, and his smile could light up a room.

Betty's life revolved around caring for her son, and she became an expert at managing his care. She knew every medication, every dosage, and every treatment plan by heart. But despite her knowledge and dedication, she couldn't stop the disease from progressing.

When Derrick passed away at the age of 12, Betty was devastated. She had spent seven years caring for her son, and now he was gone. The grief was overwhelming, and Betty struggled to find meaning in her life without Derrick by her side.

In the weeks and months that followed, Betty found solace in her memories of Derrick. She continued to write about her experiences, and her blog became a source of comfort for others going through similar struggles. She also began volunteering at a local hospice, using her experience as a caregiver to help others in need.

Through it all, Betty never forgot the lessons she learned from her son. She learned to cherish every moment, to find joy in the small things, and to never give up hope. Though she would always carry the pain of losing her son, she knew that his memory would live on in the love and compassion she shared with others.

Overcoming Grief

Some common strategies that caregivers can use to help them cope with grief:

Seek support: It can be helpful to talk to others who have gone through similar experiences or to seek support from a therapist or counselor.

Practice self-care: Taking care of oneself is important during times of grief. This can include getting enough sleep, eating well, and engaging in regular exercise.

Engage in meaningful activities: Participating in activities that bring joy and fulfillment can help caregivers feel more positive and hopeful.

Create a memorial: Creating a memorial, such as a photo album or a scrapbook, can help caregivers keep the memory of their loved one alive.

Allow time for grieving: Grieving is a natural process, and it can take time. It is important to allow oneself to feel the full range of emotions that come with grief.

Caregivers may also experience anticipatory grief, or the sense of loss that comes with knowing that their loved one's condition will continue to deteriorate over time.

It is important to note that there is no "right" way to grieve, and everyone's experience is unique. It is important to be patient with oneself and to seek help if needed.

How to Handle Grief in Full-time Caregivers

Handling grief in full-time caregivers can be challenging, and it is essential to approach it with sensitivity. Be aware of signs of grief in yourself or others and encourage self-care and seeking support. Avoid judgment or criticism and instead, provide emotional support and offer to help with caregiving tasks.

Grief among full-time caregivers is a common but often overlooked topic. Identifying and addressing the causes and effects of grief can lead to better mental and physical health for both caregivers and care recipients. It is essential to seek support and prioritize self-care to overcome grief successfully. Full-time caregiving can be emotionally and physically exhausting, but taking care of oneself and seeking help can make the process more manageable

The Difference Between Mourning and Grieving [1]

Grieving and mourning are a part of life after loss — allowing yourself healthy strategies for coping and supporting someone else after a loss can be tough but worth it.

Losing someone you love or supporting someone through a loss is not an easy task. If you've lost someone close to you, you may feel overwhelmed, sad, and alone. If you're supporting someone through a loss, you may not know what to say or how to help them.

Grief and mourning are a part of what occurs during a loss. Though they're similar, grief and mourning have different meanings.

Loss can mean many different things; you may grieve someone who has passed, mourn the loss of a relationship, have a job or financial loss, or lose important things. You don't just "get over" losing someone or something.

Allowing space for yourself to express and feel your emotions and reaching out for support can be helpful after experiencing a loss. No one person reacts or copes with grief and mourns a loss in the same way.

What is grief?

Grief is the emotional response to a loss. There are various ways in which you may respond to grief after a loss. The grief response solely focuses on emotions.

There are five stages of grief:

- denial
- anger
- bargaining
- depression
- acceptance

These five stages don't have to occur sequentially, and you can be in multiple stages of grief at once. You may experience many emotional reactions to grief, such as:

- shock
- increased anxiety
- disbelief or denial
- distress
- loss of appetite
- insomnia
- anger
- sadness

One review from 2022Trusted Source suggests that most people that have experienced a loss recover from the grief within a year of the loss. But this view may be limited because they don't define what "recovering" from grief means.

Those who have difficulty adapting to the loss may have complicated or prolonged grief.

In the Diagnostic and Statistical Manual of Mental Disorders, 5th edition (DSM-5), persistent complex bereavement disorder occurs after a period of intense emotional pain that lasts at least one year.

During complex bereavement disorder, you may experience emptiness, helplessness, and an intense longing for someone you have lost.

What is mourning?

Mourning is the outward response to grief. In other words, it's how you express grief after experiencing a loss and how you adapt to grief after a loss. Cultural and religious traditions and customs may be a part of mourning.

For example, a funeral or celebration of life after someone passes is a ritual of mourning. Other practices of mourning after someone passes may include:

- sharing positive memories of the person
- planting a tree or flower in their memory
- donating to an organization they were a part of
- starting a foundation to raise awareness of a specific condition
- praying

Anything that expresses grief that isn't precisely the emotional reaction is a part of mourning.

How grief and mourning differ

Now that we have defined grief and mourning, let's look at how they differ. Grief deals with the emotions surrounding the loss of someone or something. Mourning is how you express that grief.

Grief occurs during the mourning process, and mourning occurs during the process of grief.

If you're dealing with a significant loss, you may fluctuate in your emotions. Sometimes the grief you experience may be difficult, and other times, you may have moments of acceptance.

If you've lost someone, you may experience things in your daily life that remind you of that person.

For example, if you hear a song that the person you lost would have loved, that may evoke a grief response and cause you to become emotional. If you play that song in their honor, this is a mourning response.

[1] Mourning vs. Grief: What's the Difference? (psychcentral.com)

Medically reviewed by Lori Lawrenz, PsyD
— Written by Marissa Moore on April 5, 2022

Frequently Asked Questions: (FAQ's)

Is it common for full-time caregivers to experience grief?

Yes, it is common for full-time caregivers to experience grief due to the emotional attachment and stress of caregiving.

Can grief affect the physical health of full-time caregivers?

Yes, grief can lead to physical symptoms such as headaches, stomachaches, and fatigue.

What is the best way to overcome grief as a full-time caregiver?

Prioritizing self-care, seeking support, and taking breaks are effective ways to overcome grief as a full-time caregiver.

How can friends and family best support a caregiver experiencing grief?

Providing emotional support, offering to help with caregiving tasks, and listening without judgment can be effective ways to support a full-time caregiver experiencing grief.

Can grief improve over time for full-time caregivers?

Yes, grief may lessen with time for full-time caregivers, but the effects may vary and never completely disappear.

Chapter 4 — Regret

Regret, *as a full-time caregiver can encompass feelings of disappointment, sadness, or guilt that arise from a perceived or real failure to adequately care for a loved one. Caregivers may experience regret for various reasons, such as not being able to provide sufficient attention or support, believing they made the incorrect decisions regarding medical treatments or care arrangements, or feeling that they have sacrificed their own well-being and personal goals to fulfill their caregiving responsibilities.*

Regret is a normal and understandable part of the caregiving journey, but it can also indicate burnout or emotional distress. It is crucial for caregivers to seek support and resources to help them cope with their feelings of regret and maintain their own well-being.

Caring for a loved one can be both rewarding and fulfilling, but it can also be incredibly exhausting and stressful. Full-time caregivers face a unique set of challenges, from managing daily responsibilities to dealing with the emotional toll it takes on them. One common struggle that caregivers experience is regret. In this article, we will discuss the causes, effects, signs, and ways of overcoming the regretful feelings that full-time caregivers may have.

Causes of Regret

Taking care of a family member can have a negative impact on both your mental and physical health, which can lead to feelings of regret. Here are some common reasons why caregivers may experience regret:

Lack of Support: When caregivers do not receive support from their family and friends, it can make the caregiving journey even more challenging. This lack of support can result in feelings of loneliness and isolation, causing caregivers to regret not having someone to turn to for emotional support.

Missed Opportunities: Providing 24/7 care leaves little time for other activities, such as work, hobbies, and social outings. Caregivers may regret missing out on these opportunities and feel like they have lost a part of their own life.

Financial Strain: Providing full-time care can be expensive, leading to financial difficulties. Caregivers may regret not being able to provide better care due to financial constraints.

Why Did I Volunteer?

Anthony had always been a family man, so when his Uncle Angelo fell ill and needed a full-time caregiver, he didn't hesitate to volunteer. His brother Paul and sister Maria, who lived nearby, also offered to help. At first, everything went smoothly, and the siblings took turns caring for their uncle.

However, as time went by, Paulie and Maria became more and more involved in their own family affairs, leaving Anthony to shoulder the bulk of the caregiving responsibilities. Anthony found himself spending long hours taking care of his uncle, which left him little time for his own family or friends.

One day, Anthony's frustration boiled over, and he confronted his siblings about their lack of support. "I can't do this alone anymore," he said. "I need your help. You can't just leave me to take care of Uncle Ange by myself."

Paulie and Maria were taken aback by Anthony's outburst. "We have our own families to take care of," Paulie said. "We can't just drop everything to take care of Uncle Angelo."

Maria chimed in, "And what about all the times you couldn't help us because you were taking care of him? We've all had to make sacrifices."

But Anthony was not appeased. "I understand that, but I feel like I'm the only one who's been taking care of Uncle Ange lately. It's not fair."

The argument continued for some time, with neither side willing to compromise. In the end, Anthony felt overwhelmed and bitter. "I wish I never volunteered for this," he said regretfully.

Eventually, things reached a breaking point when Anthony fell ill due to the stress of taking care of their uncle. This was a wake-up call for Paulie and Maria, who finally understood the immense sacrifices Anthony had been making. They decided to step up and take on more caregiving responsibilities, giving Anthony the opportunity to rest and recuperate.

As time passed, the siblings grew closer as they went through this experience together. They learned how to communicate more effectively and provide support for one another. Although taking care of their uncle remained a difficult task, they faced it as a united family.

Effects of Regret

Regret can take a significant toll on the physical and emotional well-being of caregivers.

Here are some common effects of regretful feelings:

Depression and Anxiety: Regret can lead to feelings of hopelessness and helplessness, resulting in depression and anxiety.

Loss of Joy: Caregivers may lose the joy they once found in the care they provide, leading to feelings of dissatisfaction and resentment.

Burnout: Regretful feelings can contribute to caregiver burnout and make it difficult to continue providing care.

Signs of Regret in Caregivers

It is essential to recognize the signs of regret in caregivers to address the issue effectively. Here are some common signs:

Withdrawal: Caregivers may withdraw from social engagements and activities they once enjoyed.

Irritability: Caregivers may display signs of irritability, anger, and frustration.

Emotional Distress: Caregivers may experience emotional distress, such as depression and anxiety.

Overcoming Regret

Overcoming feelings of regret in full-time caregivers can be challenging, but it is possible. Here are some ways to overcome regret:

Seek Support: Caregivers should seek emotional support from family and friends, a therapist, or a support group.

Focus on the Present: Caregivers can reduce feelings of regret by focusing on the present and accepting the situation as it is.

Practice Self-Care: Caregivers should prioritize self-care and practice activities that promote physical and emotional well-being, such as exercise, meditation, and hobbies.

How to Handle Regret

Handling regret requires self-reflection and seeking support. Caregivers should acknowledge their regrets and take steps to address them. Seeking support from a therapist or support group can provide additional guidance and coping strategies.

Regret is a common struggle among full-time caregivers, but with the right coping strategies, it is possible to overcome these feelings. Seeking support, focusing on the present, and practicing self-care can contribute to long-term improvement in caregiver well-being. It is essential to recognize the signs of regret and take steps to address these feelings, such as speaking with a therapist or joining a support group. Caring for a loved one is a challenging task, and it is essential to prioritize self-care and seek support in the process.

Frequently Asked Questions: (FAQs)

What are some common causes of regretful feelings in full-time caregivers?

Common causes include loss of personal freedom and identity, financial strain, and the emotional toll of caring for someone with a chronic illness or disability.

Can regretful feelings in caregivers lead to substance abuse?

Yes, regretful feelings may contribute to substance abuse. Caregivers experiencing stress and regret may turn to drugs or alcohol as a coping mechanism.

Can therapy help caregivers overcome regret?

Yes, therapy can help caregivers overcome feelings of regret. A therapist can offer guidance, coping strategies, and emotional support. Therapy can also provide a safe space for caregivers to process and address their regrets.

Can caregivers have feelings of regret when they choose to provide care?

Yes, caregivers may still experience feelings of regret, even when they choose to provide care. It is common to feel overwhelmed and regretful in challenging situations.

Can regretful feelings in caregivers lead to abuse of their loved ones?

Regretful feelings may contribute to neglect or abuse in rare cases. However, seeking support and addressing feelings of regret can prevent neglect or abuse from occurring.

Can therapy help caregivers overcome regret?

Yes, therapy can help caregivers overcome feelings of regret. A therapist can offer guidance, coping strategies, and emotional support. Therapy can also provide a safe space for caregivers to process and address their regrets.

Life with Harold – No Regrets

Ellen sat in the dimly lit living room, the soft hum of the old clock on the wall filling the silence. It had been several years since her mother passed away, yet the absence felt as fresh as the day it happened. Her father, Harold, had been lost since that moment, a once vibrant man lost and alone.

Every morning, Ellen would rise early, the sun barely breaking the horizon, and prepare breakfast for her father. She would make his favorite—scrambled eggs with a sprinkle of cheese and a side of toast. As she carried the plate to the table, she felt a mix of tenderness and sadness. She loved her father dearly, yet it pained her to see him so hollow.

"Good morning, Dad," she said gently, setting the plate down in front of him.

Harold looked up; his eyes clouded with memories. "Morning, Ellie," he replied, his voice gravelly and distant. He reached for the toast but paused, staring out the window as if expecting to see her, his beloved wife, waving back at him.

Ellen watched him, a lump forming in her throat. "I thought we could go for a walk today, maybe to the park?" she suggested, hoping to coax a smile from him.

He shrugged; his gaze still lost in the past. "I don't know, sweetheart. I'll let you know later."

It was a delicate dance, this caretaking. Ellen had taken on the role of both daughter and a quiet caregiver, trying to lift her father from the shadows of grief without pushing him too hard. Every day was a battle against the weight of sorrow that hung over their home.

But Ellen was determined. After breakfast, she gently nudged him into a light jacket and led him outside. The crisp autumn air was refreshing, and leaves danced around them, vibrant hues of orange and gold. She hoped the beauty of the day would spark some joy in her father.

As they walked, Ellen began to share stories— funny tales from her childhood in Brooklyn, snippets of her life now. She watched for the flicker of recognition in his eyes. Occasionally, he would chuckle, and she would bask in that warmth, even if it was fleeting.

"Do you remember the time I tried to bake a cake and it turned into a disaster?" she asked, grinning.

Harold chuckled softly, the memory barely surfacing. "You nearly set the kitchen on fire," he replied, a hint of a smile creeping across his face.

"That's right! And Mom didn't stop laughing for a week," Ellen said, feeling the bond between them strengthen, even if just for a moment.

As they continued their walk, they reached the park, where children played, and couples strolled hand in hand. Ellen's heart ached for her father, imagining the joy he once had with her mother, their laughter echoing in the same spaces.

"Remember the time we fed the birds here?" he said, surprising Ellen. "Your mother brought breadcrumbs."

Ellen's heart soared. "Yes! She loved doing that. She said it made her feel like a kid again."

For the first time in a long while, they shared a genuine laugh. The heaviness of his grief lightened, if only for the moment. Ellen felt a flicker of hope, a reminder that there were still memories to be cherished, even in the shadow of loss.

As they headed home, Ellen took her father's hand, holding it tightly. "Dad, I know it's hard. I miss Mom too. But we're in this together, okay?"

Harold looked down at their entwined fingers, and for the first time in years, he nodded. "You're right, Ellie. I need to try."

That evening, as they settled into their usual routine, Ellen felt a warmth in her heart. She knew the road ahead would still be challenging, filled with ups and downs. But for the first time in a long while, she felt they were moving forward, together.

Ellen knew that while grief never truly goes away, they could carry it together, learning to find joy in the small moments, honoring the love that had always bound their family. And in that love, they could both begin to heal.

As the leaves turned from vibrant orange to a muted brown, Ellen noticed small changes in her father that began to worry her. He would often forget where he placed his glasses or repeat the same questions within the span of a few minutes. At first, she brushed it off as normal signs of aging, but when he misidentified her as her mother one afternoon, the weight of reality began to settle heavily on her heart.

After a visit to the doctor confirmed her worst fears—Harold had early-stage dementia—Ellen felt the ground shift beneath her. The diagnosis was a cruel twist in their journey, one she had hoped they could navigate together. The news hit her like a wave, leaving her gasping for air.

In the weeks that followed, Ellen stepped into a new role—one of a caregiver in a world that was becoming increasingly foreign to her father. She transformed their home into a safe haven, labeling drawers and cupboards with simple words and pictures, creating a map of familiarity in a landscape of confusion.

"Dad let's go through some old photos today," she suggested one afternoon, hoping to spark recognition and joy. She spread out the albums on the living room floor, the scent of aged paper mingling with the faint aroma of coffee.

Harold sat beside her; his brow furrowed in concentration. They flipped through the pages together, and Ellen pointed out pictures of family gatherings, birthdays, and vacations. "Look, this was your 70th birthday party! You blew out all the candles."

Harold squinted at the photograph, a hint of a smile forming. "I remember... there was a cake, right?"

"Most definitely! And you insisted it was the biggest cake ever made," Ellen laughed, hoping to coax more memories to the surface.

But as they flipped to the next page, the moment passed, and Harold's eyes clouded over again. "I can't recall... who are these people?"

Ellen's heart ached. "They're your friends, Dad. From the neighborhood. You all went fishing together every summer."

His face fell, and Ellen felt the familiar sting of tears. "I wish I could remember," he murmured, looking lost.

"It's okay, Dad. We'll make new memories together," she reassured him, though she felt the weight of despair creeping in.

As days turned into weeks, Ellen quickly learned the importance of patience and presence. Some days were easier than others. On good days, they would take walks in the park, and she would listen to him recount stories from his youth. On other days, his frustration would bubble over, and he'd lash out, confused by his own mind.

One evening, while preparing dinner, Ellen heard her father calling for her from the living room. She rushed in, only to find him staring blankly at the wall. "Are you okay?" she asked, her heart racing.

"I can't find her," he said, his voice trembling. "Where's your mother?"

Ellen knelt beside him, taking his hand in hers. "Mom isn't here, Dad. She's... she's in our hearts. Remember? We carry her with us."

"I thought I saw her," he whispered, tears welling up in his eyes.

"It's alright to miss her," she said softly, her own tears spilling over. "I miss her too. But I'm here, and I love you."

As winter approached, Ellen found herself researching more about dementia, connecting with local support groups, and seeking advice from professionals. She learned to embrace the good days and to navigate the storms of confusion and anger with grace.

As the holidays approached, Ellen decorated their home, filling it with lights and ornaments. She played their favorite carols, hoping to evoke memories of past celebrations. One evening, as they sipped hot cocoa, she asked, "What's your favorite holiday memory, Dad?"

Harold paused, his eyes darting as if searching for the answer. "I... I remember the lights. Your mother loved the lights."

Ellen's heart swelled. "She did! We used to drive around the neighborhood and look at everyone's decorations. Do you remember that?"

A flicker of recognition sparked in his eyes. "Yes! The blue ones... she loved those."

"Exactly! Let's do that again this year. Just you and me," Ellen suggested, her heart racing with hope.

And so, they bundled up and drove through their neighborhood, the car filled with laughter and warmth. The twinkling lights illuminated their faces, each glow a reminder of love and connection.

Ellen vowed to cherish each day with her father, to embrace the present, and to hold tight to the love that would guide them through the darkness ahead.

The winter months dragged on, and with them came an unsettling shift in Harold's behavior. Ellen had noticed it slowly, like the creeping chill in the air that signaled the approach of a storm. The gentle moments they once shared began to be overshadowed by confusion and frustration.

One morning, as Ellen prepared breakfast, she heard a loud crash from the bedroom. Her heart raced as she rushed down the hall, only to find her father on the floor, having tried to get out of bed without help. Panic surged through her as she knelt beside him.

"Dad, what happened?" she asked, her voice trembling. "I just wanted to get my slippers," he mumbled, his eyes wide with a mix of embarrassment and defiance.

"Let's get you back up," she said gently, but as she tried to lift him, he resisted, pushing her away with surprising strength. "I can do it myself!" he insisted, but his body gave way, and he fell back down with a thud.

Ellen felt a wave of helplessness crash over her. "Please, Dad. Let me help you," she pleaded, but he was lost in his own world, fighting against the very help he needed.

It became a routine—a painful cycle of falls and futile attempts to regain his independence. Each time, Ellen would lift him off the floor, her back aching and her heart heavy with worry. Despite her best efforts to create a safe environment, Harold's determination to care for himself often led to disaster.

Then came the day that changed everything. Ellen had just stepped out of the shower when she heard a loud, desperate cry. She rushed to the bedroom, only to find her father sprawled on the floor, his face contorted in pain.

"Dad!" she shouted, fear gripping her. She knelt beside him and saw that he wasn't moving his leg.

"I can't… I can't move," he gasped, his face pale.

Ellen's heart raced as she dialed 911. The ambulance arrived within minutes, and as they lifted Harold onto a stretcher, the gravity of the situation sunk in. He was rushed to the hospital, and the doctors confirmed the worst: he had broken his hip.

Ellen spent the next three weeks by his side in the hospital, feeling the helplessness claw at her insides. She watched as he struggled through physical therapy, his spirit waning with each painful attempt to regain his strength. The once vibrant man who had shared laughter and stories was now a shadow, confused and angry.

"Why can't I just go home?" he would ask, his frustration boiling over. Ellen would stroke his hand, fighting back tears. "We'll get you home soon, Dad. Just a little more time."

But deep down, the weight of her father's suffering pressed heavily upon her. One night, as she sat in the dim hospital room, watching the steady beep of the heart monitor, a single thought echoed in her mind: "I want out. I just can't do this anymore"

The words hung in the air, unspoken yet undeniable. She wanted out of the endless cycle of pain and confusion, out of the role of caregiver that felt more like a prison every day. She wanted her father back—the man who had taught her to ride a bike, who had danced with her in the living room, who had always been her rock.

But she couldn't voice those feelings. She had to be strong for him. It was a burden she had willingly taken on, but as the days wore on, the toll was evident. Ellen felt the guilt of her feelings to get out of the situation creep into her spirit, along with the grief of watching her father sink slowly into a mere shadow of his existence.

On the day Harold was finally discharged, Ellen helped him into the car, his expression a mix of relief and apprehension. "It'll be good to be home," he said, though Ellen could see the uncertainty in his eyes.

Back in their familiar surroundings, Ellen tried to restore a sense of normalcy. She set up a makeshift recovery area in the living room, complete with his favorite chair, pillows, and a blanket. But as the days turned into weeks, Harold's behavior grew increasingly erratic. He became more uncooperative, refusing to follow through with the physical therapy routines, insisting he could manage on his own.

"Dad, you need to do this," she urged one afternoon, holding out his therapy band. "It'll help you get stronger."

"I don't need your help!" he shouted, his voice echoing through the house. "I can take care of myself!"

Ellen felt the sting of tears, but she swallowed hard. "I know you can, but it's okay to accept help. It doesn't mean you're weak."

"You don't understand!" he roared, throwing the band across the room

The words cut deep, and Ellen stepped back, her heart aching. "I just want you to be safe," she said, her voice barely above a whisper.

In the silence that followed, the weight of their reality settled heavily around them. Ellen felt the frustration and despair rise within her, a storm that threatened to break. She wanted to scream, to cry, to let the world know how hard this was. But instead, she took a deep breath, trying to steady herself. But the thoughts of continuing this grievous routine birthed feelings of regret. "Why did I ever take on this responsibility?" Those words he spoke in anger and desperation, "I'm not your child! I'm your father!"

As the weeks wore on, she knew she needed to find a better way to navigate this new chapter. She reached out to support groups, seeking advice and connection with others who were facing similar struggles. Slowly, she began to carve out time for herself, allowing moments of respite amidst the chaos, even if it felt selfish.

One evening, as she sat on the porch watching the sunset, she felt a flicker of hope. This was a journey neither she nor her father could control entirely, but it was a journey they could face together.

The winter light filtered through the frosted windows, casting a muted glow in the living room where Ellen sat, her heart heavy with worry. Harold had become a shell of the man he once was, retreating into himself like a flower wilting in the cold. He spent most days in silence, his defiance manifesting in angry outbursts and stubborn refusals to engage with anything or anyone.

Ellen felt as if she were navigating a minefield, each day a new challenge. Bathing him had become a struggle; he resisted her attempts, his once gentle demeanor replaced by a fierce need for independence that he could no longer maintain. She often found herself exhausted, both physically and emotionally, as she battled not only his declining health but also the relentless tide of his frustration.

As the weeks passed, she recognized that his hygiene and overall well-being were slipping. It was a painful realization that gnawed at her conscience. She tried to enlist the help of home health aides, but

Harold would hardly cooperate, often lashing out at anyone who entered their home. It was a cycle of despair that left Ellen feeling isolated and defeated.

One evening, after a particularly difficult day, Ellen sat on the edge of her bed, tears streaming down her face. The weight of guilt pressed down on her chest. She remembered the vibrant man who had taught her to ride a bike, who had danced with her at family celebrations, and now he was trapped in a body that was failing him.

It was then that she made the heart-wrenching decision to research nursing homes. She knew it was best for him, that the level of care he needed was beyond what she could provide. She hoped to find a place that could offer him the dignity and support he deserved.

After visiting several facilities, she finally found one that seemed suitable, though it was an hour away from her home. The staff was warm and welcoming, the environment clean and bright. But as she sat in the parking lot afterward, she felt a wave of nausea wash over her.

Placing him in a nursing home felt like a betrayal—an admission that she could no longer be the daughter he needed. But desperation clawed at her, and after much agonizing deliberation, she made the decision.

The day of the move was shrouded in a heavy silence. Ellen packed his belongings, trying to focus on the positive aspects of the new environment. "You're going to meet new friends, Dad," she said, forcing a smile. "And they'll take good care of you."

But Harold only stared back at her, his eyes clouded with confusion. When she helped him into the car, he looked bewildered, as if he were being taken somewhere he didn't want to go.

At the nursing home, after settling him in, the reality of the situation hit her like a punch to the gut. He looked so small in that room, surrounded by unfamiliar faces and the sterile smell of antiseptic. As she said goodbye, tears welled in her eyes. "I love you, Dad," she whispered, hoping to convey the depth of her feelings.

He looked at her, and for a fleeting moment, she thought she saw recognition. But then it was gone, replaced by an expression of sorrow that mirrored her own. "I'll be alright," he said, though they both knew it was a lie.

After she left, the days turned into weeks, and Ellen tried to convince herself she had made the right choice. But every night, guilt wrapped around her like a heavy blanket, suffocating and relentless. She visited as often as she could, but Harold faded further away each time. He was often unresponsive, lost in a world that felt increasingly alien to him.

Then, one afternoon, Ellen received the call that shattered her world. Harold had passed away. The nursing home staff had failed to notice his decline, and by the time they found him, it was hours too late Rigor Mortis had set in, and the funeral director's words echoed in her ears like a haunting refrain.

"I'm so sorry, but in order to prepare him for the casket, we'll need to break both legs to straighten them out."

Ellen's heart felt as if it had been ripped from her chest. The image of her father, the man who had once been so full of life and laughter, reduced to a body that needed such treatment was unbearable.

For months, guilt consumed her thoughts. She replayed every moment, every decision, wondering if she could have done something differently. Should she have fought harder to keep him at home? Should she have found a different facility?

As she sat in her empty living room, surrounded by memories of her father, Ellen felt the weight of her loss pressing down on her. The sorrow was a constant companion, a reminder of the love that had once filled their home.

Eventually, she sought solace in support groups, connecting with others who had faced similar struggles. They shared their stories of love, loss, guilt, grief and regret and in those moments, she began to find a flicker of understanding.

Grief was not a linear journey; it was a tangled web of emotions. Slowly, she learned to forgive herself for the choices she had made, to honor her father's memory not with regret but with love.

Ellen began to create a memorial in her heart, celebrating the man he had been—the father who had taught her resilience, who had shown her the beauty of life. She kept his favorite photographs around the house and shared stories of him with friends, allowing his spirit to live on through her.

Though the pain of his loss would never fully fade, Ellen found strength in the love they had shared. The journey had been difficult, but she was learning to navigate the waves of grief, finding a way to honor her father while also allowing herself to heal. And in that healing, she discovered a deeper understanding of love—a love that endured, even in the face of loss.

Reflecting on her journey with Harold, Ellen recognized the richness of a life fully embraced. Despite the challenges she faced in the end, she felt a profound sense of fulfillment—truly, a life lived without regrets.

Helplessness

Helplessness in full-time caregivers refers to a feeling of powerlessness or lack of control over a situation where they are responsible for the care of another person. Full-time caregivers often provide care for individuals who are unable to care for themselves due to age, illness, or disability. Caregivers may feel overwhelmed and unable to cope with the challenges they face. This can lead to a sense of helplessness, where caregivers feel like their efforts are not making a significant difference in the well-being of the person they are caring for.

Feeling of Helplessness in Full Time Caregivers

Taking care of someone with a chronic illness or disability can be an overwhelming and challenging task. Full-time caregivers often struggle with feelings of helplessness, which can lead to physical, emotional, and mental exhaustion. On this topic, we will discuss the causes, effects, signs, and ways of overcoming helplessness in full-time caregivers.

Causes of Helplessness in Full-time Caregivers

Lack of Support: Many caregivers feel isolated and unsupported. They may not have anyone to discuss their feelings with or may not receive enough help from family, friends, or medical staff.

Inadequate Resources: Caregivers may struggle to access essential resources, such as healthcare, information, and financial assistance.

Physical and Emotional Demands: Caring for someone full-time can be physically and emotionally draining, especially if the caregiver has to perform demanding tasks like lifting, bathing or managing medications.

Effects of Helplessness in Full-time Caregivers

Stress and Anxiety: Caregiving can be a significant source of stress and anxiety, which can lead to a higher risk of depression, chronic illness and a diminished quality of life.

Physical Exhaustion: Caregiving can cause physical exhaustion, leading to feelings of fatigue, headaches, muscle pain, and other health problems.

Emotional Distress: Frequent exposure to suffering, illness and death can cause significant emotional distress in caregivers.

Signs of Helplessness in Full-time Caregivers

Loss of Interest: Caregivers who feel helpless may experience a lack of interest in activities they once enjoyed.

Fatigue and Burnout: Caregivers may feel emotionally and physically exhausted and experience signs of burnout, such as irritability, anger, and feelings of hopelessness.

Poor Physical Health: Frequent exposure to illness may lead to caregivers neglecting their own health, leading to a higher risk of illness.

Overcoming Helplessness in Full-time Caregivers

Seek Support: Caregivers who feel helpless should seek support from others. This can include family, friends, support groups or healthcare professionals.

Prioritize Self-care: Caregivers should prioritize their self-care by establishing a routine that includes time for rest, exercise, healthy eating and relaxation strategies.

Ask for Help: Caregivers should not be afraid to ask for help whenever necessary. Help can come in the form of respite care, home health services, or hired assistance.

Results Over Time

Over time, many caregivers find that the skills they develop throughout their caregiving journey can be useful in other areas of their lives, such as improved communication and empathy.

How to Handle Helplessness in Caregivers

Practice Mindfulness: Caregivers can practice mindfulness to be more present and focused, decreasing feelings of overwhelm and increasing their ability to cope effectively.

Trust Yourself

Caregivers should trust themselves and their instincts. The role of caregiver requires making difficult decisions, and following intuition can be the best course of action.

Take Breaks Regularly

Caregivers should take regular breaks to recharge, and the person they care for can receive the best care when the caregiver is also at optimal health.

In conclusion, caring for someone full-time can be challenging, overwhelming, and emotionally draining. Caregivers can experience feelings of helplessness, which can worsen without proper support, care, and treatment. It is crucial for caregivers to seek support, prioritize self-care, and ask for help whenever necessary. Techniques such as mindfulness, trusting oneself, and taking regular breaks can go a long way in combating feelings of helplessness and burnout.

It's OK to Ask for Help!

Juanita stood in the middle of her empty living room, the walls echoing the laughter and chatter of the life she once knew. The sleek lines of her designer furniture felt cold and foreign, reminders of a world she had left behind. Just months ago, she had been a successful manager at an exclusive ladies' clothing store in the King of Prussia Mall, poised for a promotion to regional management. Her days were filled with fashion shows, meetings, and the thrill of retail; her nights, with friends and the vibrant social life that came with her success.

But everything changed with a single phone call. Her mother had suffered a heart attack, and suddenly, the vibrant life Juanita had built began to crumble.

She rushed to the hospital, her heart racing not just from fear but from the suffocating weight of responsibility. As the doctor explained her mother's condition, Juanita felt the walls closing in around her. It was a moment that would redefine her existence.

The decision to leave her job was gut-wrenching. She had always dreamed of climbing the corporate ladder, of proving herself in a world that often-overlooked women. But as she sat by her mother's bedside, she knew she had to prioritize family over ambition. She gave her notice, vacated her condo, and moved back into her childhood home. It was a sacrifice she thought she could handle—a temporary measure, she told herself.

But weeks turned into months, and the weight of caregiving began to suffocate her spirit. Juanita found herself waking up each day to a routine that left little room for her own needs. She managed her mother's medications, cooked meals, and helped with physical therapy. Each task felt monumental, and the joy from her old life faded like a distant memory. The vibrant colors of her past were replaced by the muted tones of exhaustion.

As the days wore on, Juanita felt a gnawing regret. She had sacrificed her career, her social life, and even her sense of self for a duty that was becoming increasingly overwhelming. She loved her mother, of course, but this was not the life she had envisioned—a life of caring for someone who needed her yet feeling increasingly helpless. The walls of her childhood home felt more like a cage than a sanctuary.

One day, while sitting on the porch, staring at
the same view she had known all her life, her phone
buzzed. It was a message from her friend Claudia,
who had been checking in on her. "I know this is
hard, Juanita. Have you looked into in-home care
services? Medicare can cover it. You don't have to do
this alone.

Juanita stared at the message, her heart racing. The
thought of bringing a stranger into her home made
her uneasy, but the idea of sharing the burden was
like a light breaking through the clouds. She spent
the rest of the afternoon researching options, her
fingers moving quickly across the keyboard, her heart
pounding with a mixture of hope and fear.

That evening, she called a local agency. The friendly
voice on the other end of the line reassured her,
explaining how the service worked, the qualifications
of the caregivers, and how Medicare would cover the
costs. It felt surreal, as if someone had lifted a weight,
she didn't even know she was carrying.

As the days passed, she arranged for a caregiver to
come and assist her mother for a few hours each day.
When the first caregiver arrived, Juanita felt a mix
of anxiety and relief. She watched from the kitchen
as her mother and the caregiver chatted, laughter
spilling out into the air. That laughter was a sound
Juanita hadn't heard in weeks.

For the first time in months, she felt a flicker of
her old self emerge. With the burden of constant
care lifted, Juanita began to rediscover the joys of her
life outside caregiving. She reconnected with friends,

began to explore new job opportunities, and even found time to indulge in her love for fashion again.

In the weeks that followed, the sadness that had consumed her began to dissipate. Juanita realized that caring for her mother didn't mean she had to sacrifice her own happiness. It was possible to find a balance, to love and support her mother while still nurturing her own dreams.

As she walked through the mall one afternoon, the familiar sounds of laughter and chatter washed over her. She felt a renewed sense of purpose, knowing she could navigate both worlds. Juanita smiled, not just for her mother, but for herself—a woman who had chosen love over regret and found strength in vulnerability.

Frequently Asked Questions: (FAQs)

How do I know if I am experiencing caregiver burnout?

Some signs of caregiver burnout include physical and mental exhaustion, feeling overwhelmed, and loss of interest in activities.

How can I prioritize self-care when I am always busy with caregiving duties?

It's crucial to schedule time for self-care and ask for help from family and friends or hire a professional caregiver to free up time.

Is there any financial assistance available for full-time caregivers?

Yes, some programs offer financial assistance for caregivers. Check with your community resources or healthcare providers for more details.

Can support groups really make a difference in managing caregiver stress?

Yes, support groups offer emotional support, practical advice, and a sense of community that can help manage caregiver stress more effectively.

How does mindfulness help caregivers manage their stress?

Mindfulness practices, such as meditation, help reduce stress by promoting relaxation and present-moment awareness. It can increase resilience and boost the overall well-being of caregivers.

Is it normal to feel guilty or ashamed for needing help as a caregiver?

No, it is not unusual to feel guilty or ashamed of times as a caregiver. However, it is crucial to acknowledge these feelings and seek help whenever necessary.

THE CAREGIVERS BILL OF RIGHTS

The Components of the Caregiver's Bill of Rights

The Caregiver's Bill of Rights is made up of five components that empower caregivers to take care of themselves while providing care to their loved ones.

These rights include:

• *Right to Self-Care*

Caregivers have a right to take care of their physical and emotional health needs. Taking care of yourself is essential to ensure that you remain healthy and are capable of providing care in the long-term.

• *Right to Seek Assistance*

Taking care of someone with a health issue or disability can be challenging, and caregivers need to have access to resources and support when they need it. This right provides caregivers with the opportunity to seek assistance from family members, medical professionals, and community resources.

• *Right to Balance*

Caregiving can be a full-time job, and it's essential to achieve a balance between your responsibilities as a caregiver and your personal life. This right encourages caregivers to seek out activities that bring them joy and fulfillment outside of caregiving.

• *Right to Respect*

Caregivers have a right to respect from their loved ones and medical professionals. Their opinions and views on the care of their loved ones should be considered when creating care plans.

• *Right to Information*

Caregivers need to have access to information about their loved ones' medical condition and care plan. This right encourages healthcare professionals to provide caregivers with information that will help them provide the best care possible.

How the Caregiver's Bill of Rights Can Improve Caregiving

Implementing the Caregiver's Bill of Rights can improve caregiving in several ways, including:

Improving Overall Health and Well-being

Caregivers who practice self-care and seek assistance when needed are more likely to remain healthy and avoid burnout.

Improved Caregiver-Recipient Relationship

Caregivers who have access to resources and support are better equipped to provide quality care to their loved ones, improving the caregiver-recipient relationship.

Reduced Caregiver Burnout and Stress

Taking care of your physical and emotional health needs can reduce stress and burnout, making caregiving more manageable in the long-term.

The Caregiver's Bill of Rights provides a framework that supports family caregivers and promotes their rights to take care of themselves while caring for their loved ones. These rights can improve care recipients' health outcomes, improve caregiver-recipient relationships, and reduce caregiver stress and burnout.

If you are a caregiver, make sure you familiarize yourself with these rights, and don't be afraid to advocate for your needs. By taking care of yourself, you can provide better care for your loved ones.

Maximizing the Guide into your Journey

To maximize this guide, we recommend:

- Dedicate regular time to reflect on the information and your experiences.

- Use the guide as a resource for support.

- Connect with support groups or online communities for encouragement.

- Celebrate small victories and acknowledge your growth.

Remember, overcoming guilt, grief, and regret is a gradual process. Be patient with yourself, practice self-compassion, and utilize the resources to enhance your mental health and overall well-being.

My hope is that this book has illuminated the emotional struggles of full-time caregivers. In this guide, I've explored the causes and effects of guilt, grief, and regret with suggestions for overcoming them.

The importance of self-care is emphasized, and I recognize the vital role caregivers play in our society. The insights shared here aim to empower caregivers to address their emotional challenges and prioritize mental health.

This guide serves as a resource for adopting a mindful approach to self-care and fostering supportive communities, helping care-givers improve their well-being and care for their loved ones.

We aspire for this guide to contribute to a healthier society for caregivers. Caregivers DO Matter!

Contact R. Lee Moore, Sr.

For Book Signings & Speaking Engagements:

RLeeMooreSr@gmail.com

(844) 246-2200

www.RonaldLeeMooreSr.com

R. Lee Moore, Sr.
295 E. Swedesford Road, #288
Wayne, PA 19087

www.**Moore**BooksR.us

www.**Moore**BooksR.us

OVERCOMING...

A Caregiver's Guide

Explore the emotional struggles and challenges faced by full-time caregivers, delving into the causes, effects, and strategies for overcoming feelings of frustration, anger, stress, guilt and exhaustion. These guides also underscore the vital importance of self-care.

It is essential to acknowledge the immense role that caregivers play in our society, highlighting their personal sacrifices and the profound impact they have on the lives of those they care for. The knowledge shared will serve as a guide for caregivers to embrace a mindful approach to self-care and cultivate supportive communities, fostering improved well-being and enhanced care for their loved ones.

The ultimate goal of this book is to contribute to a healthier, more compassionate society that values the crucial work of caregivers.

Remember, *Caregivers DO Matter.*

OVERCOMING

- Frustration, Anger, & Exhaustion
- Lonliness, Abandonment, & Depression
- Anxiety, Worry, & Stress
- Guilt. Grief, & Regret

www.MooreBooksR.us

Think Feel Speak Write — Do 2.0

A Path Toward Realizing Your Purpose

Many of us are frustrated, confused, and lack enthusiasm; just going through the motions in life. We have settled for the world's definition of who we are instead of agreeing with God who has created us on purpose.

In this book are insights and stories that offer a fresh outlook on how these principles can impact your journey. You too may find that as you Think, Feel, Speak, Write, and DO purposefully, you can live a fulfilling life as God created you to live, with purpose.

Get started today!

www.onecreativemindllc.com/think2 or thinkfeelspeakwritedo2.com

---

"Why Won't They Just Die!"

"Emotional turmoil of Caregivers often goes unnoticed."

When a caregiver experiences the thought, "why won't they just die!" they are not actually expressing a wish for the death of their loved one. It's used in a time when the caregiver feels that they've reached their limit; in a moment of over-whelm, frustration and desperation, where they feel like they're running out of options.

www.whywonttheyjustdie.com

www.ingramcontent.com/pod-product-compliance
Lightning Source LLC
Chambersburg PA
CBHW051234120626
46547CB00013B/1644